IN THE KINGDOM

In
the
Kingdom

Jonathan Blake

LOST VALLEY PRESS

Lost Valley Press
An Imprint of Satya House Publications
P. O. Box 122
Hardwick, MA 01037

lostvalleypress.com

ISBN: 978-193587447-8

*book designed by Sarah Bennett
shbennettbookdesign.com*

*Cover painting: "Creekside," by Vanessa Varjian
vanessavarjian.com*

MANY THANKS to the editors of the following journals where many of these poems or versions of such appeared:

Amoskeag; Beloit Poetry Journal; Blueline; Cavan Kerry Press's The Waiting Room Reader: II; Crosswinds Poetry Journal; Monadnock Writer's Anthologies: poems of Longing; Mud poems; Poetry East; Noh Place Poetry Anthology; The Vermont Review; The Worcester Review.

for my mother and my father
&
for Elizabeth

CONTENTS

I

the black cry of crows
grows softer and softer
across the open sky

Sunflowers standing in November

Like the sculptures of Giacometti

Three short rows of slender stalks casting
Cold shadows in the last light of afternoon

Perfect heads bowed as if awaiting
Terrible orders of instruction

Think of any history when the living are gathered
Into the village square suddenly certain of dying

The long march into winter soon to begin

Prayer

How to explain my wonder

The single engine of a small plane

The bright purple finch perched, still,
Keeping vigil as his stone-gray mate
Warms the tiny world of her egg

The perfume of lilac in morning
Like a woman whispering in your ear

What it means to hear spring

The still shadow of the small jade
On the white wicker table
Signing the spirit of god

Into the perfect circle of darkness
One wasp moves into cool brick

No sadness in the gardens

The imperfect perfection of what sings
In the rows of furrowed shadows—
The newly tilled earth: line after wandering line

New basil standing up in the sun

The white hair of the ghost
Of my father thinning the chard

My mother's strong hands tying the tomatoes

One crow gleams in the dead limbs
Of a tree close to the compost

What is divine and what is
Ordinary; what sings
And what is still

The slow red dance of geraniums
On the sunlit terrace a beautiful mystery

The bronze wings of the butterfly
Coming to rest on the worn
And weathered banister

The crooked stairs that lead down
And into the garden

In the valley

Wherever you are is a monastery.

— Charles Wright

Dark wings of hemlock slow in the morning
Wind; saplings of maple and oak

A sudden war along the tops of trees:
One crow banished by two

And then—
A return to the singing
In the forest of the far shore

A stillness in the valley
Blemished by these words—

Yet how else to say
There is a luminous yellow-green
In the newly hayed fields
Of the horizon

The young men have moved on
To new pastures

That the sky is the color of wet slate
Above those fields

The air so thick it shapes us
Like the breath of god

And the wind—gently rocking
A boat waiting
On silver water

How to love the earth

Lie down with your shadow,
That long darkness that stretches
Across the yellow-gold of the newly
Mown hayfield. Breathe deep of that
Odor. Be patient and still.
Wait for the birds who will
Descend like a great dark cloud, who
Will cover you with their warmth,
Who will pick your bones clean.

Devotion

Like the burnished body
Of Jesus worn smooth
With kisses on the cross
My grandmother carried.

Aria

Again and again she returns
To the beginning, altering
The notes that come from the darkness
At the center of the cabin
Until there is no mistaking
Her grief, until the music sustains
A beautiful sadness and she is able
To find her way to what is glorious and magnificent.
Each morning her voice across water
Is a sorrow we take pleasure in.
We sit close to the stony shore
And practice our weeping.
She never sings in sunlight,
Never at night; her children remain
Patient at the end of the dock,
Poles in the pond, running to her
When she emerges, shaking
Her red hair free, laughing
As she pulls them close,
The terrible gods of tragedy
Again, somehow and miraculously, appeased.

After love and the storm

I pull a thin sheet
Over your naked, dreaming body.
Linger looking down at you.
Summer rain drips from the trees.
Sunlight breaks. The birds return to singing.

Waiting for Elizabeth to waken

Because she is still
Sleeping I will linger
Close to the dark pond
With paper and pen
Waiting for words

Diving like the kingfisher
Into his reflection

And rising
If the gods should smile

With something that gleams
And sustains

Ceremony

All morning each of them comfortable
With the quiet made by the wind.
Birds sing deep in the pines.
The few words between them like music:
Careful octaves of human joy
That even the gods refuse to disturb.
They drift under great planets
Of cumulus and out again
Into the white August sun.
One by one the roses they toss
Fan away from the old rowboat,
Red petals loose themselves
On green water, dragonflies
Holding fast to slow blossoms.
There is no explanation for their happiness.
The flowers spinning lazily away.
The silence between them ceremonial.
Each of them happy and alone
Together in the small boat only
Two days before the loneliness
Of their late summer return
Down from the mountains
Into the noise of the world.

Remembering the T'ang

Tonight
The moon
Is a paper
Lantern set
Adrift on the
Slow black
Current
Of the pond

On the far shore

It is from this distance
I must love her, keeping
Her pure, not spoiling her
With the sweet ruin of my heart.
The music of her French voice
Darkens my sorrow but soon
I am lost to the moment
She suddenly turns her head
Astonished again by the world—
Golden hair flashing, her white
Summer shift the color of marble
Against the cool shadows that lean
Out from the pines, bright against
The brown of her bare feet.

She stands close to the water,
The distance between us less
Than our years; she looks long
Into the valley, listening
Perhaps as I listen to the single
Call of a crow or the steady trill
Of the crickets coming from the wet
Darkness of the tall grass, listens
To the bare-chested boys laughing
In the far hills as they load
The wagons with hay—listens,
Locking it all away before

She boards the plane home
To her mother who waits
Wondering after one month's time
If this is the summer she will return
A young woman who knows
The warm breath of an eager boy
In the hollow of her throat.

I have no such wonder, needing only
What lives in the quiet wind come
Down from the green hills, sunlight
Warm and strong against my body,
Desiring only this distance
Between us, her beauty lighting
The late afternoon I will lock away
In the bare winter rooms of my heart.

August moonrise

Like a young woman
Averting her gaze
The pale pearl face
Of the moon rises
Over black pines—

Becomes less coquettish
In the open sky

Her lost twin trembles
On dark water

Meditation

I wake at dawn
To water slapping stone.
Look down on the wild
Iris bending in the wind.
Sunlight flames across the black-pine horizon.
From the next room the old
Breathing of my parents still asleep.
I am beyond the middle of my life.
Seeking a name for it.
Believing in each day there is wisdom.

The fisherman and the poet

What the river says, that's what I say.
— William Stafford

Here in the Kingdom
We are brothers
In waiting: the man
Standing in his skiff
In the cove below:
The whip whistle of his line,
The percussion of his lure
On sunlit water.

On the hill above
I turn the pages
Of Bill Stafford's poems
Waiting: pen and pad
Close by like a net
To be lifted from the dark—
Holding the gleaming
And thrashing body.

Voyage: *The long marriage*

How long has it taken them
To arrive at this understanding?
Him at the prow of their skiff:
Tall, thin, white beard lit by the sun,
Looking out like an explorer,
Reeling his taut line from the water.

Her turning the quiet motor
Every now and then with her left foot,
Seated on the pedestal chair to the rear,
Setting their direction, bending
Her head again as if in prayer
When she returns to the open book
In her lap: the two of them
Moving slowly into shadow,
Into light, shadow, and light again.

All morning like this.
No words between them.

Remembering the legend of Li Po's death

Night darkens the river
Two moons shining

Opening one more bottle of wine
I walk to the water's edge
And pull my boat ashore

II

night comes on like a wash
of ancient ink

Months after her death

Suddenly the smell
Of wild dill through
The open window
Above the kitchen sink.

What comes next
Does not surprise you.
A small trembling begins.
Like the wind that is wild,
She lives in you.

Again, the soul

It is the body that tethers us
To the world, of that I am certain.
It is the soul that puzzles me.
Does it grow larger with our steady determination
Toward death? Grow ripe like the fine August
Garden with the suffering we provide?
With love and work and music?
Become the shine of what is important
In our lives? And if so, what then?
Released, will it still hear the crows at dawn?
Smell the bitterness we knew staining
Our hands after tying the tomatoes?
Will it remember the kindness of women?

Or does the soul diminish each day?
A slow distillation into what is pure.
Our growing old the alchemy: a reduction of
    particulars.
Our sitting close to the Vermont pond at dusk,
Happy with the smell of water and the arc of swallows;
How we are puzzled by our gratitude for that sudden
Loss in the middle of our life,
Rolling away wet and spent from love
In the thick July heat;
How we managed the terrible ache
That accompanied our witness
To the world's suffering. Can we say our ordinary
Lives burn in the furnace of that living,

That what is to be found in the ashes
After is without imperfection?
Is it enough to name it mystery or essence?
Compare it to the shadows growing into
Darkness at dusk? Can we call it the season
Of lilac delicately alive on the soft night wind?
Without us, what will its life be then? What song will
    it know?
What longing?

Song for Natalie

Tired and overcome
With the delicate perfume
Of lilac, I sink into my chair.
Cold wine and the pale spring moon.

Suddenly, Natalie, my neighbors'
Young daughter is running
Into the coming darkness,
Shouting angrily that she is old
Enough, old enough, old enough.

She has not noticed the moon.
Is not drunk with lilac and the dying
Lavender sky; does not know that she is not
Old enough, but that with each step
Into the terrible darkness she moves closer
To that moment when she too will stagger
Into the face of beauty,
The heart knowing its burden,
When the brilliant moon
And the sweet lilac and the quiet night
Are enough.

Autumn leaves: *A prelude*

Bill Evans: piano; Scott Lafaro: bass; Paul Motian: drums

A man listens again to the great trio
And imagines the long curve
Of Evans' back bent to the piano,
His burden the slow and careful music
Of what is difficult in our lives.

His wife is away again.
He makes dinner for one:
Small shank of lamb;
The ratatouille she prepared
Before departing. New radishes
From the garden.

One candle burns as he writes
To an old friend who lives near.
The sky has turned
The cool indigo of late summer.
What he feels in his heart
Is not new but changes him
Once more.

When Evans stops playing
There is a moment of loneliness:
In the stillness of the shadows
Beyond the long open windows,
The first soft rain
Of September begins.

I am at it again

I am at it again, leaning
Into my wingchair, writing
One more letter in lamplight, listening
To Miles and Mingus, to Billie, Betty
And Bird, to Lambert, Hendricks and
Sweet Annie Ross.

I am at it again John Coltrane,
Hearing Ornette and Lacy, El Zabar and Pharoah,
O the Creator does have a Master Plan, Master
Plan Master Plan....

I am at it again Pops, from ragtime to no time, caught
In the wonderous sphere of Thelonius, *Straight, No
        Chaser,*
Blue Monk, Epistrophy, Crepescule for Nellie;
Ruby, Yes, *Ruby, my dear,* I am at it again.
I am at it again wise Sonny Rollins,
Tender Mr. Evans, growling slow and languid
With your bone Roswell Rudd. I am
At it again.

Waking after a long night of rain

I have nothing to be sad for.
Even death.
My lover wakes me
With a kiss.
The garden is no longer hard and dusty.
The tomatoes grow heavy and shine.
Morning sunlight fans
Through the small leaves
Of the old beech and from the dark
Water of the shadows
A solitary cricket calls.

There are no gates
To his world.
Only song.

Taking shape

We don't choose love—
It chooses us.
Is too big for us
In the beginning
But takes our shape
In time. Like a fire
That reduces itself to red heat.
Like a storm suddenly
More than the sky
Becoming the powerful
Maples swaying like women,
Like men drunk
With love as long rolls
Of thunder move over
The valley.
Like a sudden explosion
Of swallows in the cool morning
Trying to keep form
Above the pond, finding
New shape in the dark
Shadows of the barn.
We have no control
Of the magnificence
In our lives, no determination
For what flowers in us
Like wild blossoms
That are fragrant

In the darkness of the spirit,
For the tenderness that casts delicate shadows
In the white light of the heart.

Understanding the old heart

In candlelight.
Sitting on the stone porch
With tangled geraniums
And trembling shadows.
Night rustling the spent lilac.
Elizabeth sighing
Before she whispers her weariness
And goes off to bed.
Alone and lonely and happy
With my wandering mind.
Moonlight occasionally.
Dinner plates resting
On the torn tablecloth.
Dogs barking in the valley below.
The fragrance of lilies just opened:
The strong smell of potted basil.
How we come to believe in our life.
Enter the quiet rooms of the heart attentive,
As if for the first time.   Making our way slowly.
Finding something sweeter than ambition.

Castle Street August: *Worcester, Ma.*

After great rolls of thunder
And the flash-crack of lightning,
Children lean from
The brick bay windows
Of tenement brownstones
Listening to the rain.

Early afternoon: *After oysters and cold wine in Worcester*

Black sandals in hand
She steps from under the eaves
Barefoot   Summer rain

Totem

For Rose

Some mornings my wife kneels in the bed
Of flowers close to the stone porch
Believing he sings to her. Like all music
His is written into the silence we carry with us.
His dark and weathered face a spirit
Carved into walnut grain.
When our neighbor moved away
She was filled with sorrow.
We found him leaning against
The granite cornerstone, a note left
Pinned to our door.

He belongs here with you.

My friend mistakes his expression
For eternal pain, eyes half closed, lips
Twisted as if just before some terrible
Song of mourning. I explain it's not the ruin
Of the soul he sees, not among the stargazers
And the wild mint, the tulips and the iris:
I tell him my wife believes a different story,
One older than the myth of our exile;
She says each garden is passage
Into paradise, this face—reminder
Of our rapture.

Visitation

Fog drifts along the black
Jagged tops of pine.
Winter rain. I sit close to the fire
Lost to the flames.
In the stillness a voice
Whispers a name I have
Long forgotten. Two sparrows
Seek shelter in the twisted heart
Of the bare lilac.
It will be months again
Before I am surprised
By the fragrance of blossoms:
Spring's last delicate chill—
The heart as if young again.

How long have I lived
With white hair?

How is it she found her way
In the dark rain?

Two lessons

Tired of my writing brush, I gazed
Out the windows.

— Po Chu I

I am alone.
She will return
In the darkness
Of late afternoon,
Weary, maybe even sad.
I will try not to be
So happy it hurts.
All day she lures
Her students back
To the board, away
From the windows,
Scolding those who
Do not pay attention.

My chair sits
Facing out over
The valley. Sunlight
On new snow.
Smoke rising from
The village chimneys.
In this empty room
The quiet of the heart.
Occasionally I will
Turn a page. Sometimes
Close my eyes.
When she returns
I will read her poems
From the T'ang.

Wang Wei writes—*What's a man of peace*
To do all day?

Tu Fu asks—*How many times in one man's life*
Can he listen to heaven's music?

Ars poetica

Hibiscus blossoms and the flower
Of the moon. Church bells echo
Into a village stillness far below.

Tonight, my students ask,
"But what is poetry?"

How do I tell them
About the quiet in the heart,
Wind stirring the trees,
My wife and I together
On the porch, no words
Between us, happy
For what grows fragrant
In the dark?

III

a calligraphy of shadows
along the moonlit path

Trying to be tender

Raising his thin
T-shirt over his head
My father asks me to change
The dressing on his back
Where death's black root
Has taken hold
Of one more mole.

It has come to this again between us:
The ritual of tender care. My hands
Now middle-aged, gently pulling
The old bandage off the soft,
Milky skin, cleaning the wound
Left by the surgeon's scalpel,
Pressing the back of my father's head
Forward so the skin will tighten,
The new bandage hold true.

What I wonder
As I pull his shirt slowly
Over my careful work
Is whose death do I
Now know better—

His or my own.

Three years after his death: *My reply*

In the stillness
Of dusk four years ago
My father called out
For me from the path
Close to the dark
Waters of nightfall.
His words were the new
Tenderness of his dying.

This morning, his voice
Rustles the leaves.

No sirens singing

All morning he wrestles growing old.
Thinks of what is lost, what is gained.
Wonders if the quiet measuring
Is the beginning of how we come to death:
A kind of equation. The body showing signs
Of weariness. The spirit growing wiser.

The November rains have stripped
The trees, and all that remains
Are the small russet fires
Of oak leaves rattling in the cold wind.
What startles him on his morning walk is the brilliance:
The stark forest beyond the fallen
Garden luminous after days of black rain.
The light blinding. As if the gods had returned.
Grass white with frost. Earth turning to stone.
The silence of no birds singing.

He thinks this is the way it will be.
Him standing alone around
The slow beating of his heart.
The shining like the last
Great light between this world
And the next. No sirens singing.
No annihilation. Simply, a doorway
Opening. Something beckoning.
Something showing the way.

Joy

Some days there is no explaining it
Like shore birds rising all at once
From the mudflats of my bones

Two horses

Thunder into the sun
At the center of the pasture.
What cries come deep
From their magnificent bodies
Fill the sky.
I love to watch them
When they first charge
From the dark barn
Into sunlight, tossing
Their great heads,
Pushing aside the strong
Spring wind.
I love to feel the earth
Tremble as they run
Along the old stone walls.
I love to walk out
Under lush maples
And watch them
Finally come to rest,
Their brown bodies shining,
Their two heads close
In the stillness they have made,
Their soft breathing
Loud enough
So I may never forget.

Vigil

Heavy flakes of snow float
Beyond the windows that overlook
The valley. The hills of the horizon
Are blue. I have forgotten what it is
I must do in this world and the voices
That trouble me are still. I grow
Old, but the winter light in my small
Room grows and fades like the breath
Of god. I do not need science to know
It enters me, lights the holy marrow
Of my bones. I am not the dark wings
Of those birds coming to rest
In the bare oak like the blind eyes
Of a woman who knows night
Comes on. No. When the long mirror
Of the world grows opaque, I am
Nothing. And nothing more.

Portrait

Each of you without words—
Your shadow and you
Standing on the moonlit path

Four

for Aimee

Seeking a truth that is absolute
A woman I know paints
The same landscape in different seasons
Simultaneously: autumnal burning
Next to the dark and tangled calligraphy
Of maple, oak against a winter
Sky: the new green promise of spring
The earth keeps and the trees of lush
Summer like the confidence of a woman
Who sits in sunlight alone waiting
For the sudden whisper of a lover
Into her turned and delicate ear.

Four landscapes and four horizons,
Each with its own longing, as if
To say here is the world's dimension,
A slanted perspective to the light
Of our wistfulness and wanting;
The skies bright and blue and infinite;
The line of the horizon a jagged darkness
That defines the heart.

Four meadows and four horses
In each: each one a chestnut,
Two with small flames of white
Between their eyes; in winter
They stand close, ragged and looking
Off, their longing equal to our own;

There is serious intention
To their solitary grazing
In the thick grass of summer's hills;
In autumn they are in love
With each other: I can hear
Their soft snorting, their quiet breathing.

Four horizons, four meadows, four horses:
I ask my friend what the truth is.
The stillness of your heart, she tells me.
The slow and serious soul of your attention.

Mock pastoral

A shifting curtain of locust
Momentarily darkens the sky.

On the horizon black smoke
From a burning city.

Close to the bend
Of a clean river a woman

Stands in sunlight folding
The warm clothing of her family,

In love with the fragrance
Of the wind, of late Spring

And the lazy songs of birds,
The shadows of long-stemmed flowers

Rising and falling upon the earth.
The city is behind her.

There has never been a day
Like this. She turns to the horizon

When her child playing
In the grass looks up;

The steady soft beating
Of the drums like a storm

Far off. Growing louder.
The earth not yet trembling.

The tethered horses still grazing.

Pilgrim

No longer the music of rain
Falling in the stone square
In Forcalquier, the stone fountain
At center spills cool water from tier
To tier. After days of darkness
Shadows deepen. The market
Takes its shape again.

Row of ripe cheeses, alley
Of saucisson, pig's feet and jellied organs;
Circle of wheat and sugars, circle
Of black chocolate. Close to the pitted
Dragons spitting water - melons
Split to the heart, peaches
And dusky plums, dark hills of cherries:
Bench of bright blossoms.

The murmur of voices begins
In the first weak light, becomes
The cacophony of bargaining
For what is needed, what is ripe.

Wet stone grows whiter as the sun
Climbs higher into the square sky.
A woman rocks an infant; eyes
Closed, face tilted into that sky,

She sings softly as her child dreams
What is warm—sunlight on his small head,
The body of his humming mother.

For centuries, I imagine, it has gone on
Like this: the village climbing the small streets
To the square; the bounty of harvest
The only story. One bell ringing far out
Across the valley: calling.

I have journeyed all my life
To get here.

The world you hold in your hands

You wake rested and rise
Into a morning where nothing
Is asked of you.
The storm has passed.
You stand on the braided rug
Peeling an orange, leaning against
The old sink as you wait for coffee.
The wind moans along the tall windows.
What visits you moves quick
As the clouds across the February sky.
Important, and not.
Red tulips opening on the walnut table.
The quiet of the house like a moment
After love, only larger.
You notice she has forgotten her cigarettes,
And you try to remember if she said
Early afternoon or evening.
Lost to the distraction of blue shadows
Across snow; The melancholy marriage
Of cello and bow softly from another room. You return
To the books and the sweet loneliness
Of your small room. Settle with orange
And coffee into the block of winter
Light that burns in your blue chair.
You dismantle the world you hold
In your hands; each segment savored,
Slowly, one by one.

A small map of melancholy

for Catherine Reed and M.B.

All morning I wander
The early winter rooms
Of our home carefully
Carrying the soft music
Of the children's sleep.

I stop and stand in the still light
Slanting through the small bay
Window that looks out
On the village green: already the skaters
Have returned: some steady
And graceful; some not.
First coffee warm in hand,
I hold in the other one poem
Given to me yesterday
By a wise friend.

Her words are a different music.
Her hands are the hands
Of her mother: delicate wings
Coming to rest on a small oak table.

My shadow stands with me, still
Against the pale wall.
The bare trees make a voice
Of the wind. I cannot stop
Remembering the dead.

IV

this life and no other

Longing: *Late spring*

for Yuka

Rain begins again.
Birds build nests beneath the eaves.
How still my heart is.

*

Last night I stood above the pond
With a woman from Japan
Who said she knew how
Poems could be found here.
This morning she returned to Boston
And I am alone, only the moon
In memory as it climbed through
The hissing trees into a sky suddenly
Free of storm. Drinking cold wine
We said the names of Basho, Buson,
Issa like a prayer. We might have said
Crickets, night birds, shadows born
From a pale northern light.
Her small body swayed like a thin
Reed in the night breeze and she leaned
Closer to a moon older than any
Homeland either of us knows.

Yuka said—

The songs of birds at dusk are poems.
Moonlight does not break the grass.

I am far from home but in Japan
The sound of distant bells
Echoes in my heart.

The day after my death

From the stillness, the sound
Of one boat being pushed
Over stones into water.
Fog lifting from the valley
As the sun grows stronger,
Shimmers on the slow
Current of the pond.
In the cool shadows
Of the pines, the measured
Mourning of doves: a single bell
Becoming a bright silence.
Far out, an oar-less boat, burning.

Late August

All day
Young men
On tractors
Turn yesterday's
Cutting of hay in the hills
Of the horizon.

What dust moves down
Through the valley
Sweetens the wind.

Solstice

How perfect the earnest
Quiet between them:
Their patience best
Without words.

Two men stand balanced
In a boat drifting
Across the brightening heavens
Reflected on the pond,
Reeling taut lines
Through silver water.

Summer's dusk

Small boats carry whispers
Close to the stony shore

Old and young, mother and son,
Two lovers drifting under a rising moon

The long slow wings of one heron
Close to the wet slate sky

Two loons an echo that quiets
The heart, drifts into the still arms
Of dark hemlock along the shore

Each cast is an act of faith:
Whip whistle hiss and then—

The old waiting, the old wonder—
What is taken as a sign

The coming night sweet
With the smell of a second cutting

The black frenzy of bats
Close to still water

Early spring: *Two a.m.*

When I stepped
Out of the cabin
To bring in another
Armful of wood to last
Until dawn, I saw her
Face broken by the new
Trees and I whispered a song
To her, startled and happy
Once more for her slow return,
Regal, rising like an angel
Of fertility out of the earth—
Suddenly, I believed again in music
And the night and love—
Still knowing that deep
In the darkness, the world
Remained, snarling, animal,
Indifferent to her shining.

Daybreak

The tall pines
Are mystics standing
In the early sun

The fog has lifted

A stillness lives in the sound
Of water etching stone

Two deer come
Down from the hills
To the shoreline to drink
In the shallow waters
That mirror their slender faces

Like lovers lifted
From the warm moon
Of their bed beneath
Dense mountain laurel

They are fragrant with the peace
Of sleep: drowsy and alert,
Ears flickering, alert and drowsy, leaning

Lightly against each other now

And again, as if love
Might make them eternal

One more meditation

There is no wisdom here
In the last light watching
The cows drift in the golden pasture
That slopes down to silver water
No wisdom in the long shadow
That lies down and leans away
From the dark barn

No wisdom—

Only the quiet heart
That wise men sometimes yearn for

Paradise

No one in the city knows
They have gone

Cusp of autumn

Heifers drifting toward the darkness
Of the farmer's barn

Far off the sound
Of geese growing louder

A pale moon rising above the pines

Loon songs

After love at dawn—
It is the loon's mournful call
That stills our slow touch

*

Louder than summer
Rain on an old tin roof:
From the gray center
Of the pond—the loon's cry

*

Even the man
Counting coins
Raises his head
To listen

*

Hearing the solitary loon
The man drifting
In his boat waiting
For the tug on his line
And the man watching
The moon climb slowly
Above the jagged pines
Are one

Growing old

Solitude tastes like opium.
—Adam Zagajewski

It was the only way
He knew. Into the mountains
And away from the noise.
Days without speaking.
His only music the rain
Falling through the trees:
One loon calling
To another at dusk.
In time, how the quiet
Became him. Dressed
As he was in the color
Of its light. Each footstep
Measured and soft and sure
Upon the earth; wandering
With the deer at night, a spirit
In the heat of the herd.
And later, with his return,
He closes the cabin door
Until he knows the quiet
Truth of the latch like an answer.
His one slow breath
Steady against the candle's flame.

What he knows when he lies
Down in the darkness
Is a radiance resembling god.

Dusk

Like the young child incessantly
Scratching the bug bites of summer,
Wandering the empty road
Toward the pull of home:
The old rowboat tightly tied
To the old dock rubs quietly
Against its mooring.

From the Kingdom: *Early spring*

All day a small fire
Speaking little we turn page
After page—happy

*

Tonight the bright moon
On the pond will fit into
My shimmering palm

*

One small fire burning
In cold rain all day, our horse
Rests one leg, another

Letter to Elizabeth away in France

I have wondered all day
What might be important enough to tell.
Certainly, last night—the gray day growing darker
And me without sadness; at dusk
Two blue herons slow and prehistoric
Along the stillness at the center of the pond.
The haunting cry of doves.
And with morning—the world brilliant again,
Whispering what grows old in us:
Points of sunlight like diamonds spilled
Across water; one slow tractor turning
Yesterday's hay where the earth meets the sky.
Summer's wind lifting the heavy branches.
To know my heart now summon the smell of water
At dawn, the quiet voices of a father and son fishing
Among the fallen trees close to the far shore,
The sudden power of last night's rain.

ONE LOVE

I want to thank Andre Juarez for forty plus years of friendship, his belief in my work, and his insistent prodding I put poems together and without whom this book would not exist. The adventure continues.

Thanks to Julie Murkette, driving force of Lost Valley Press and Satya House Publications, for her generous and kind spirit, her diligence and focus, and for her belief in the power of poems.

Thanks to the community of poets in Worcester, central Massachusetts, near and dear, far and wide who have inspired me through their own work and friendship to continue to sing the body electric.

Thanks to the musicians who always said a resounding *yes!* without hesitation whenever I wanted to incorporate music into a reading or a performance: most notably, my deep thanks to bassist Jerry Wilfong; trumpeter and percussionist Dick Hummel; and to the late John Zaganaicz, whose soul was the sound of his tenor saxophone.

Many, many thanks to Bill O'Connell for nearly forty years of friendship, correspondence, discourse, and unabated support.

Thanks to Bill, Rob Racicot and Elizabeth for wrestling the drafts of this manuscript and for their needed insight.

Thanks to Vanessa Varjian for her artistry and without whom this book would not be as beautiful.

Thanks always to my students who have always kept me alert and alive all these years and whose keen insights have always helped me to refine my own.

Greatest thanks to Elizabeth, who many years ago understood my need to sit alone and to listen and to dream, and who was infinitely patient with my doing so, and without whom most of these poems would not exist.

Jonathan Blake has been following the gospel of his heart for as long as he can remember. Writer, educator, arts activist/organizer, he makes his home in central Massachusetts.

Currently, he teaches in the English department at Worcester State University, where for the past twelve years he has hosted a round robin open reading series for students, faculty and staff and the greater Worcester County poetry community called ONE POEM. His poems and essays can be found in an array of journals and anthologies, including *Amoskeag, Atlanta Review, Beloit Poetry Journal, Brilliant Corners, Poetry East* and *The Worcester Review*. On occasion, he has the privilege of fashioning his public readings in collaboration with some of the fine jazz musicians who also call central Massachusetts home.

In 1984 my parents purchased a small log cabin overlooking a pond in a sparsely inhabited valley at the end of a long dirt road in the Northeast Kingdom of Vermont. In time, with the coming of grandchildren and great grandchildren, the family built another cabin to accommodate the gatherings of the tribe.

The rolling hills of the pastures on the horizon, the wildlife, the stillness needed for dreaming, have long been the wellspring for my writing.

In the late 1980's, after a visit to our family cabin, the poet Bill O'Connell named the place Paradise. It remains a place where poems and peace can be found.

— Jonathan Blake

Printed in the USA
CPSIA information can be obtained
at www.ICGtesting.com
LVHW092253201024
794338LV00005B/191

9 781935 874478